UKE 'AN PLAY
John Lennon

Alfred

Produced by
Alfred Music
P.O. Box 10003
Van Nuys, CA 91410-0003
alfred.com

Printed in USA.

ISBN-10: 1-4706-1002-7
ISBN-13: 978-1-4706-1002-9

 Alfred Cares. Contents printed on 100% recycled paper.

IMAGINE

CONTENTS

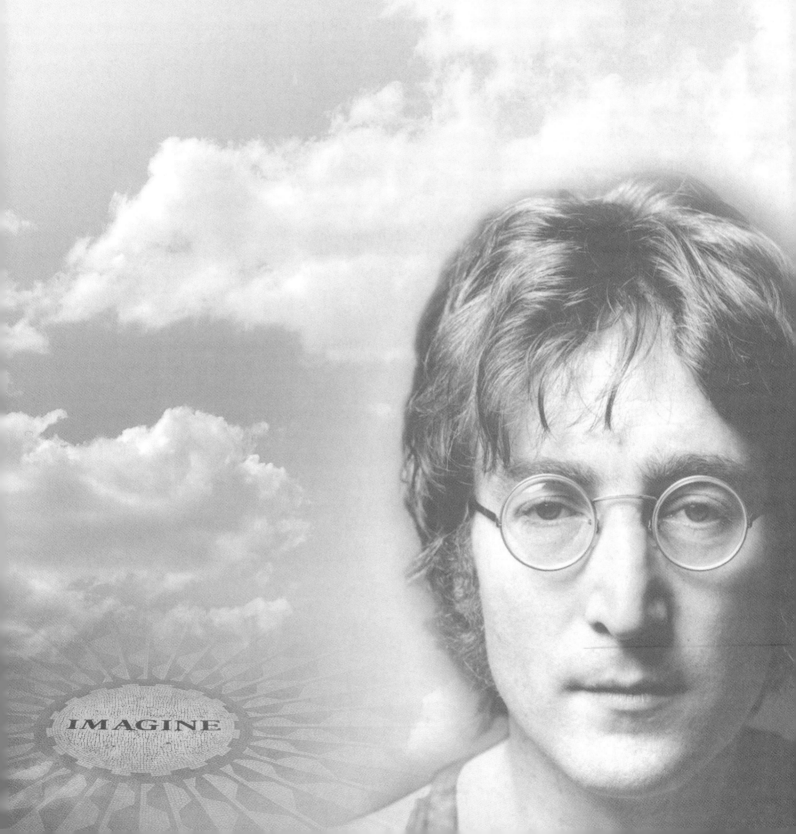

IMAGINE

BEAUTIFUL BOY
(Darling Boy)

Words and Music by
JOHN LENNON

Verses 2 & 4:
Before you go to sleep say a little prayer.
Everyday, in every way, it's getting better and better.
(To Chorus:)

Verse 3:
Before you cross the street, take my hand.
Life is what happens to you while you're busy making other plans.
(To Chorus:)

COLD TURKEY

Words and Music by
JOHN LENNON

Moderately ♩ = 114

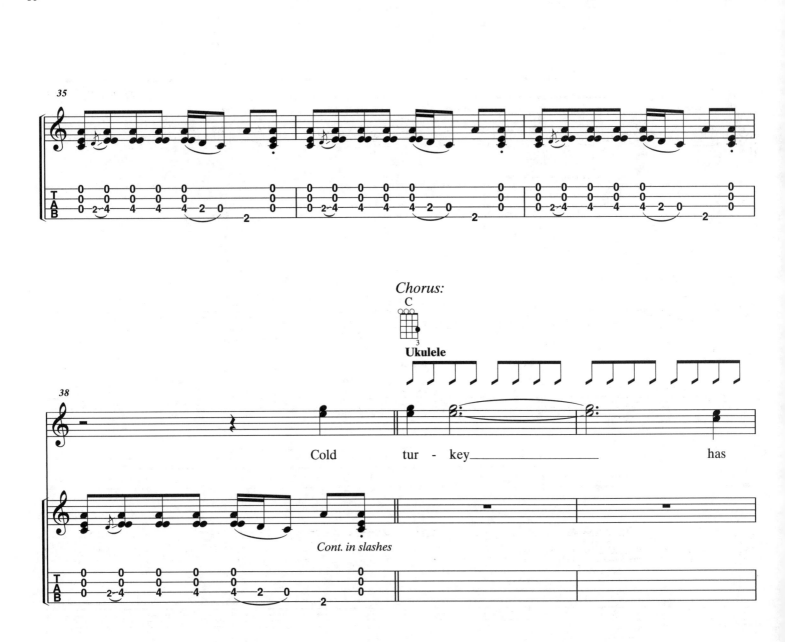

D.S. % al Coda

Coda

Outro:

w/Vocal ad lib. a crescendo of "Oh," "No," moans and screams

Repeat ad lib. and fade

Verse 2:
Body is aching, goose-pimple bone.
Can't see nobody, leave me alone.
My eyes are wide open, can't get to sleep.
One thing I'm sure of, I'm in at the deep freeze.
(To Chorus:)

Verse 3:
Thirty-six hours rolling in pain,
Praying to someone, free me again.
Oh, I'll be a good boy, please make me well.
I promise you anything, get me out of this hell.
(To Chorus:)

FREE AS A BIRD

Words and Music by
JOHN LENNON, PAUL McCARTNEY,
GEORGE HARRISON and RINGO STARR

Free_____ as a bird,____

*Sing harmony on repeat.

it's the next best thing to be,_____ free_ as a bird.

Home,_____ home and dry.

(Home._____)
*'Echo' vocal on repeat.

**Sing lower harmony on repeat only.

To Coda

like a hom-ing bird I fly,_____ as a bird on wing.

*Sing lower harmony on repeat only.

Free As a Bird - 3 - 1

14

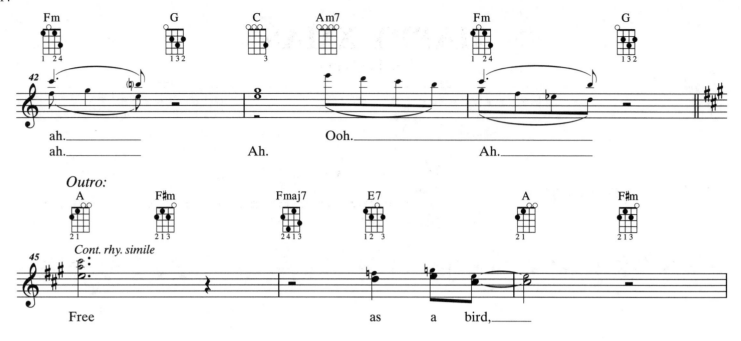

ah._____ Ooh._____

ah._____ Ah. Ah._____

Outro:

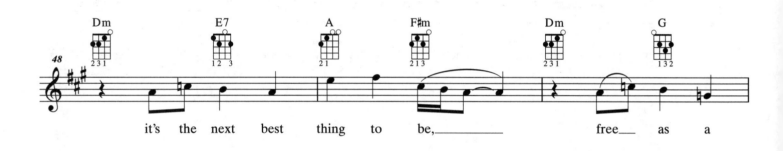

Cont. rhy. simile

Free as a bird,_____

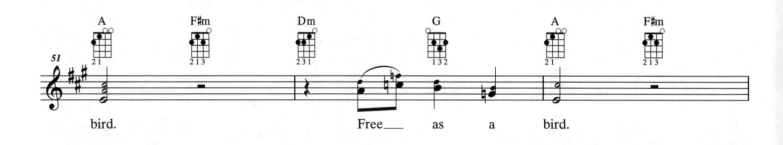

it's the next best thing to be,_____ free__ as a

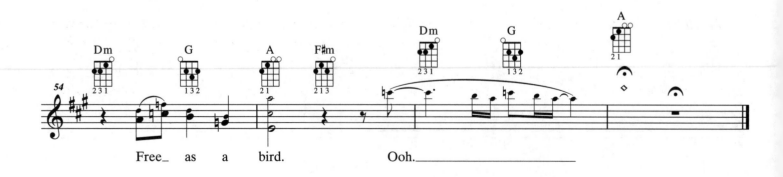

bird. Free___ as a bird.

Free__ as a bird. Ooh._____

HAPPY XMAS
(War Is Over)

Words and Music by
JOHN LENNON and YOKO ONO

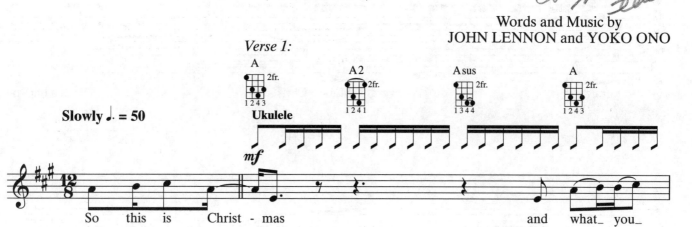

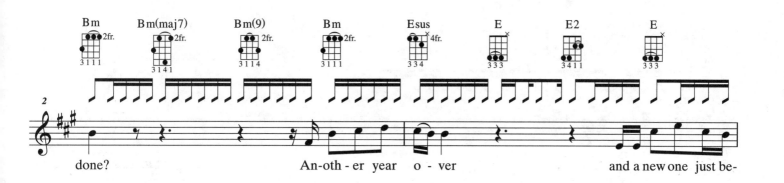

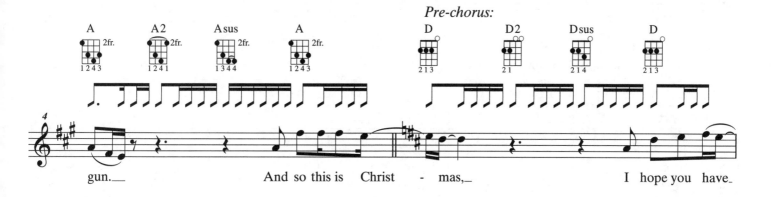

Happy Xmas (War Is Over) - 3 - 1

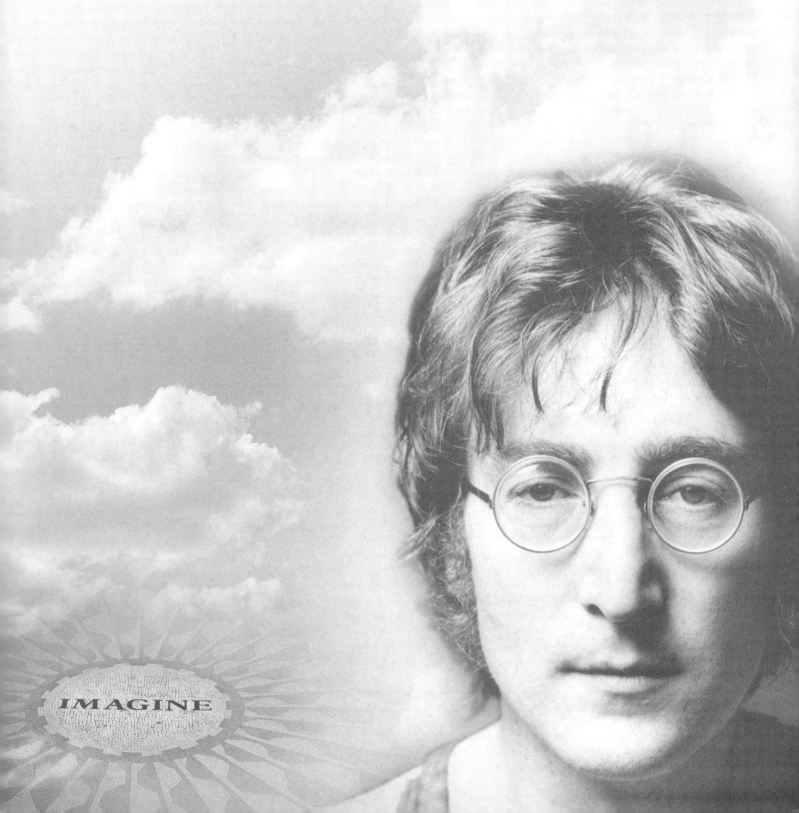

IMAGINE

I'M LOSING YOU

Moderately ♩ = 97

Words and Music by
JOHN LENNON

Bridge:

Here in the val - ley of in - de - ci - sion, I don't know___ ___ what to do, I feel you slip-ping a - way, I feel you slip-ping a - way.___

Resume. rhy. simile

I'm los - ing you,___

D.S. %al Coda

I'm los - ing you,___ well,___ now.

Coda
Chorus:
w/Rhy. Fig. 1

los - ing you.___ Ow, I'm___ los - ing you,___

Verse 5:

___ well, well, well. I know I hurt___ you then,___ but, hell, that was way___

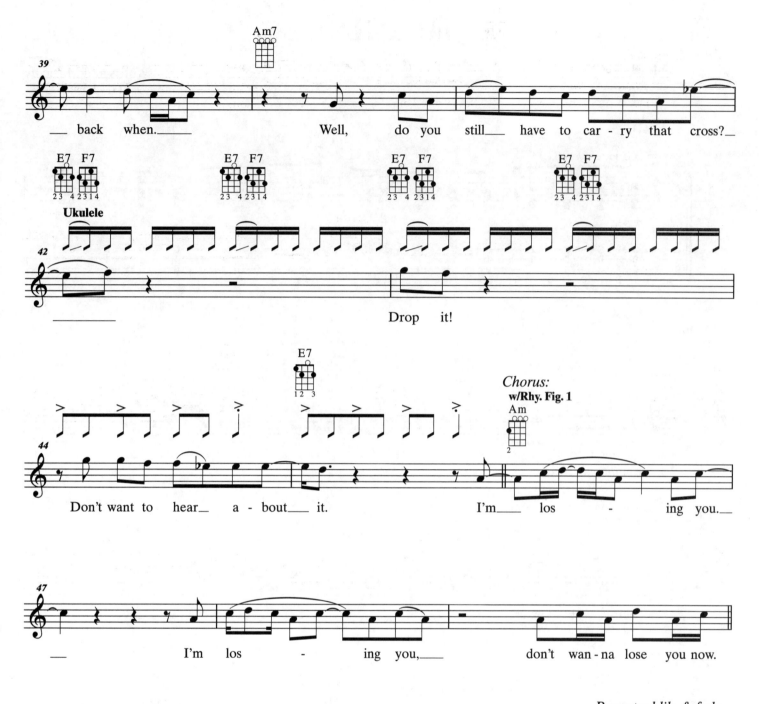

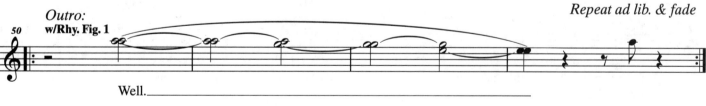

Verse 2:
Somehow the wires have crossed,
Communication's lost.
Can't even get you on the telephone.
Just gotta shout about it.
(To Chorus 2:)

Verse 3:
You say you're not getting enough
But I remind of you of all that bad, bad, bad stuff.
So what the hell am I supposed to do?
Just put a band-aid on it...
(To Chorus 3:)

12/2/2016

IMAGINE

Words and Music by
JOHN LENNON

Imagine - 2 - 1

Verse 2:
Imagine there's no countries,
It isn't hard to do.
Nothing to kill or die for
And no religion too.

Pre-chorus 2:
Imagine all the people
Living life in peace.
You...
(To Chorus:)

Verse 3:
Imagine no possessions,
I wonder if you can.
No need for greed or hunger,
A brotherhood of man.

Pre-chorus 3:
Imagine all the people
Sharing all the world.
You...
(To Chorus:)

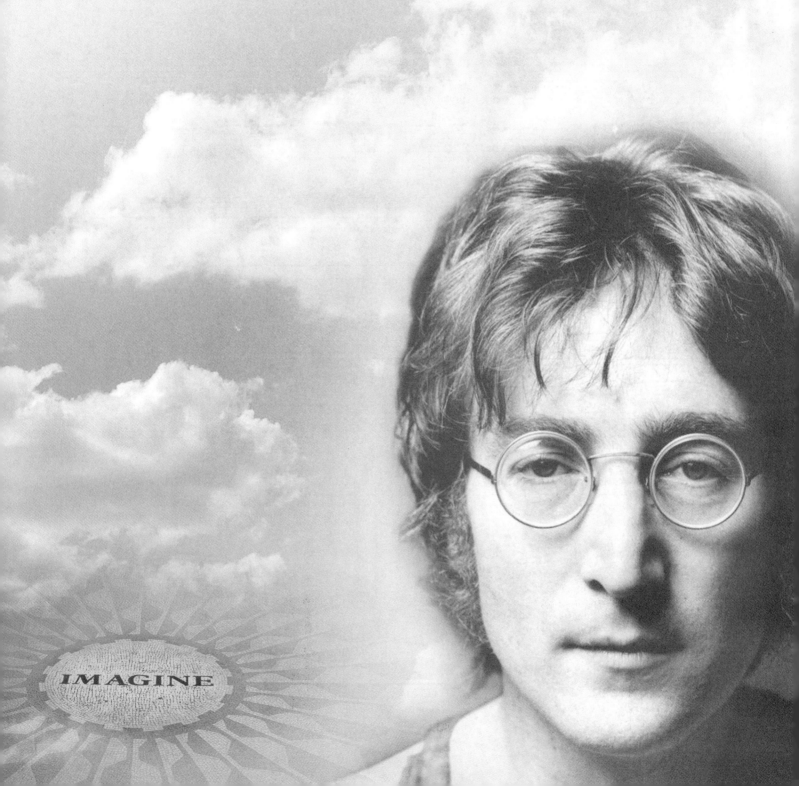

INSTANT KARMA

Words and Music by
JOHN LENNON

1. In-stant kar - ma's gon-na get you,__
2.3. *See additional lyrics*

gon-na knock you right_ on the head._ You bet-ter get your-self to-geth - er

pret - ty soon you're gon - na be dead._

What in the world you think - ing of,___ laugh-ing in the face of

love?__ What on earth__ you try'n' to do? It's

Instant Karma - 3 - 1

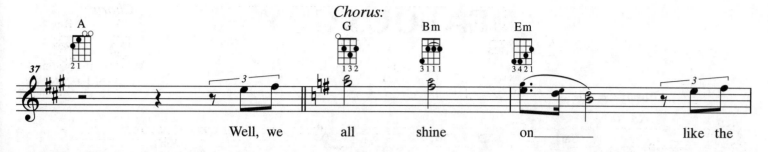

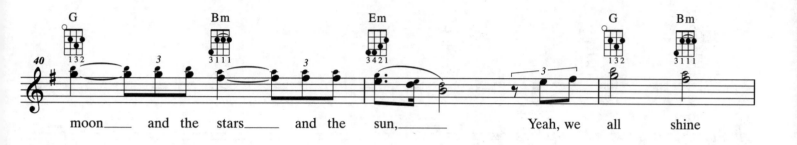

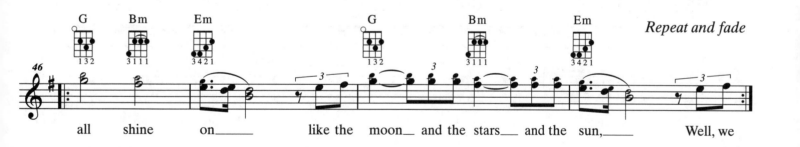

Verse 2:
Instant karma's gonna get you,
Gonna look you right in the face.
You better get yourself together, darlin',
Join the human race.
How in the world are you gonna see,
Laughin' at fools like me?
Who on earth do you think you are?
A superstar? Well, right, you are.
(To Chorus:)

Verse 3:
Instant karma's gonna get you,
Gonna knock you off your feet.
Better recognise your brothers,
Everyone you meet.
Why in the world are we here?
Surely not to live in pain and fear?
Why on earth are you there?
When you're everywhere, come and get your share.
(To Chorus:)

JEALOUS GUY

Words and Music by
JOHN LENNON

Slowly ♩ = 66
Intro:

Verse:

1. I was dreaming of the past____ and my heart_ was beat-ing
2.–4. *See additional lyrics*

fast._____ I be-gan_ to lose_ con-trol,____

Chorus:

I be-gan_ to lose_ con-trol. I did-n't mean to hurt_ you.

Cont. rhy. simile

_____ I'm sor-ry that_ I made you cry.__ Oh no,

Jealous Guy - 2 - 1

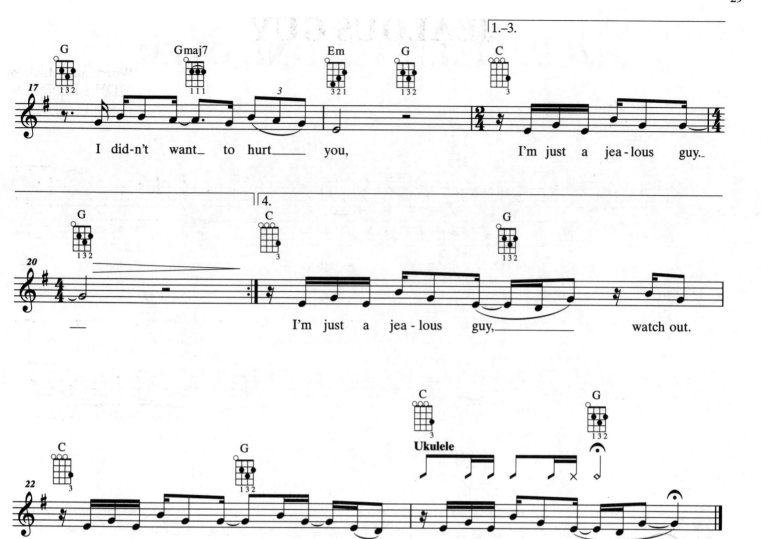

I did-n't want to hurt you, I'm just a jea-lous guy.

I'm just a jea-lous guy, watch out.

Ukulele

I'm just a jea-lous guy, look out, babe, I'm just a jea-lous guy.

Verse 2:
I was feeling insecure,
You might not love me anymore.
I was shivering inside,
I was shivering inside.
(To Chorus:)

Verse 3:
Whistling melody
(To Chorus:)

Verse 4:
I was trying to catch your eye,
Thought that you was trying to hide.
I was swallowing my pain,
I was swallowing my pain.
(To Chorus:)

(JUST LIKE) STARTING OVER

Words and Music by
JOHN LENNON

LOVE

Moderately slow ♩ = 82

Words and Music by
JOHN LENNON

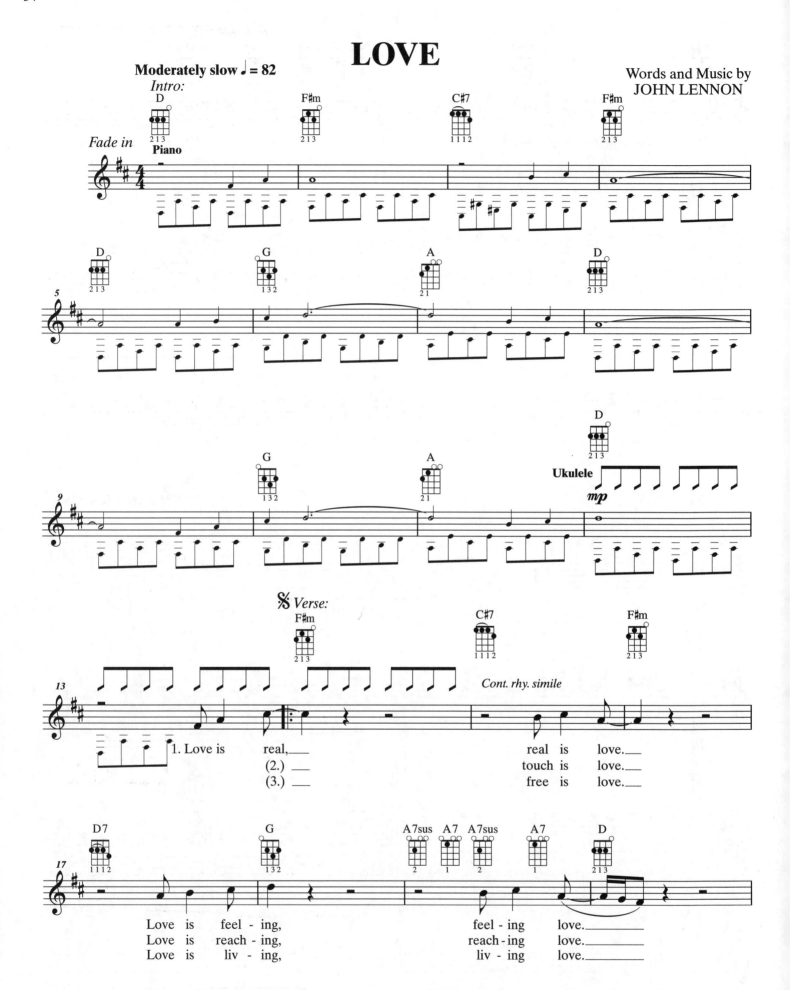

MOTHER

Words and Music by
JOHN LENNON

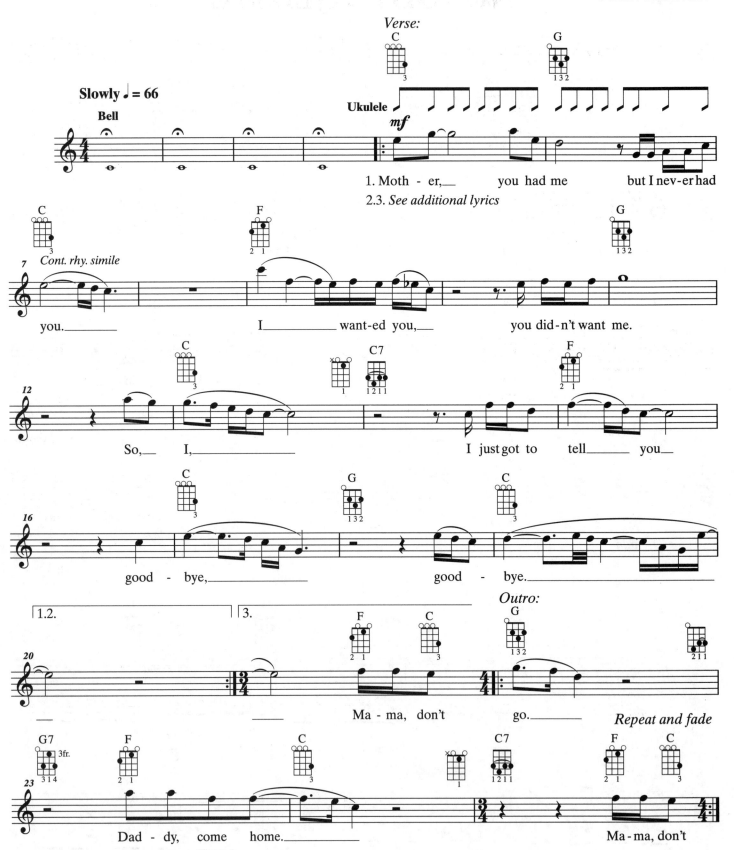

Verse 2:
Father, you left me but I never left you.
I needed you, you didn't need me.
So I, I just got to tell you goodbye,
Goodbye.

Verse 3:
Children, don't do what I have done.
I couldn't walk and I tried to run.
So I, I just got to tell you goodbye,
Goodbye.
(To Outro:)

NOBODY TOLD ME

Words and Music by
JOHN LENNON

Moderately ♩ = 118

Three, four.

1. Well,

ev - 'ry - bod - y's talk - ing___ and no one says a word.___
2. Ev - 'ry - bod - y's run - nin'___ and no one makes a move.___ Well,

Ev - 'ry - bod - y's mak - ing love and no one real - ly cares.___ There's
ev - 'ry - bod - y's a win - ner and noth - ing left to lose.___ There's a

Na - zis in the bath - room just___ be - low the stairs.___
lit - tle yel - low i - dol to the north of Kat - man - du.___

There's al - ways some - thing hap - pen - ing and noth - ing go - ing on.___ There's
Ev - 'ry - bod - y's fly - ing___ and no one leaves the ground.___ Well,
3. Ev - 'ry - bod - y's smok - ing___ and no one's get - ting high.___

Nobody Told Me - 3 - 1

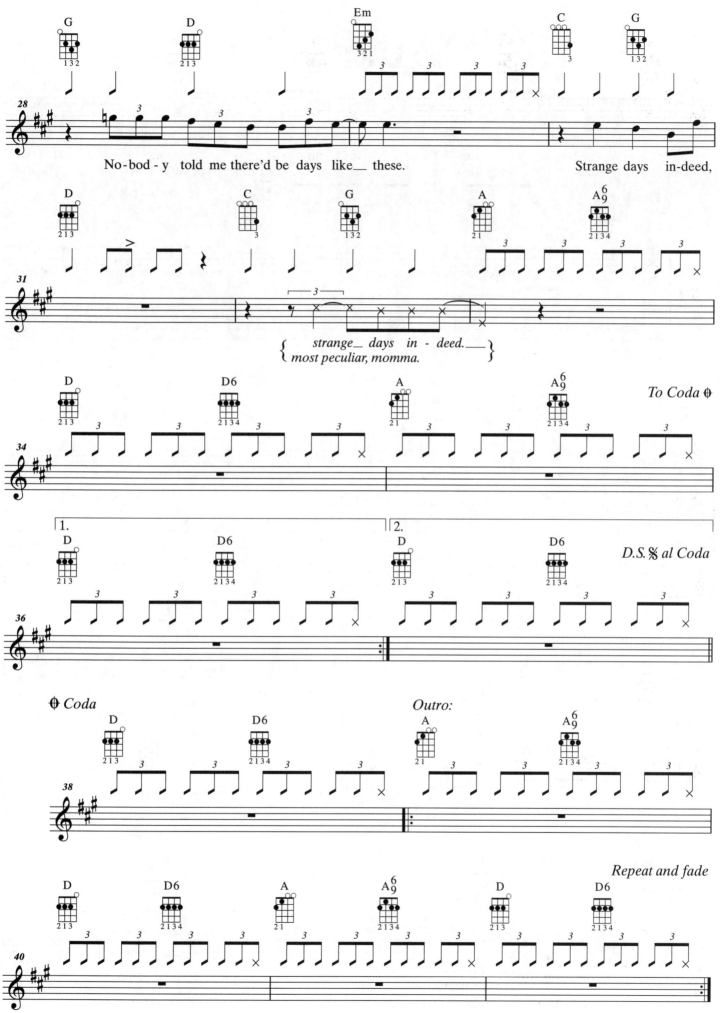

#9 DREAM

Words and Music by
JOHN LENNON

OH MY LOVE

Words and Music by
JOHN LENNON

REAL LOVE

Moderately slow ♩ = 88

Words and Music by
JOHN LENNON

All my lit-tle plans and schemes,___ lost like some for-got-ten dreams.

Seems that all I real-ly was do-in'___ was wait-in' for_ you.___

Verse 2:

Just like lit-tle girls and boys___ play-ing with their lit-tle toys,

seems like all we real-ly were do-in'___ was wait-in' for_ love.___

Pre-chorus:

No need to be___ a-lone.___ No need to be___ a-lone.___

Real Love - 3 - 1

WATCHING THE WHEELS

Moderately ♩ = 84

Words and Music by
JOHN LENNON

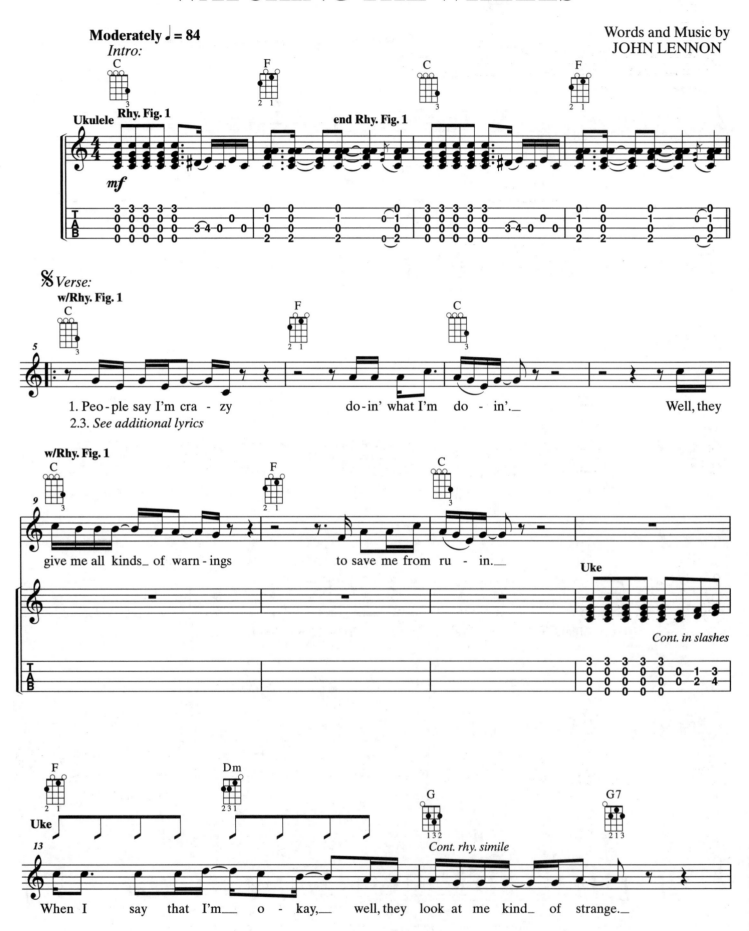

1. Peo-ple say I'm cra - zy do-in' what I'm do - in'.__ Well, they

2.3. *See additional lyrics*

give me all kinds_ of warn - ings to save me from ru - in.__

When I say that I'm__ o - kay,__ well, they look at me kind_ of strange.__

Watching the Wheels - 3 - 1

Verse 2:
People say I'm lazy, dreamin' my life away.
Well, they give me all kinds of advice
Designed to enlighten me.
When I tell them that I'm doin' fine
Watching shadows on the wall,
"Don't you miss the big time, boy?
You're no longer on the ball."
(To Chorus:)

Verse 3:
People asking questions, lost in confusion.
Well, I tell them there's no problem,
Only solutions.
Well, they shake their heads and they look at me
As if I've lost my mind.
I tell them there's no hurry,
I'm just sitting here doing time.
(To Chorus:)

WHATEVER GETS YOU THRU THE NIGHT

Words and Music by
JOHN LENNON

*Unison G notes played on 2nd and 4th strings.
See TAB for complete chord.

What - ev - er gets__ you thru the

Cont. in slashes

night,__ 'sal - right,__ 'sal - right.__

Whatever Gets You Thru the Night - 3 - 1

52

WOMAN

*To match record key, tune up a half step or Capo I

Words and Music by
JOHN LENNON

Moderately slow ♩ = 80

*Recording sounds a half step higher than written.

1. Wom-an, I can hard-ly ex-press my mixed e-mo-tions at my thought-less-ness.
2. Wom-an, I know you un-der-stand the lit-tle child in-side the man.

Af-ter all, I'm for-ev-er in your debt. And, wom-an, I will try to ex-press
Please re-member my life is in your hands. And, wom-an, hold me close to your heart.

my in-ner feel-ings and thankful-ness for showing me the mean-ing of suc-
How-ev-er dis-tant, don't keep us a-part. Af-ter all, it is writ-ten in the

cess.
stars.

Oo, well,

Woman - 2 - 1

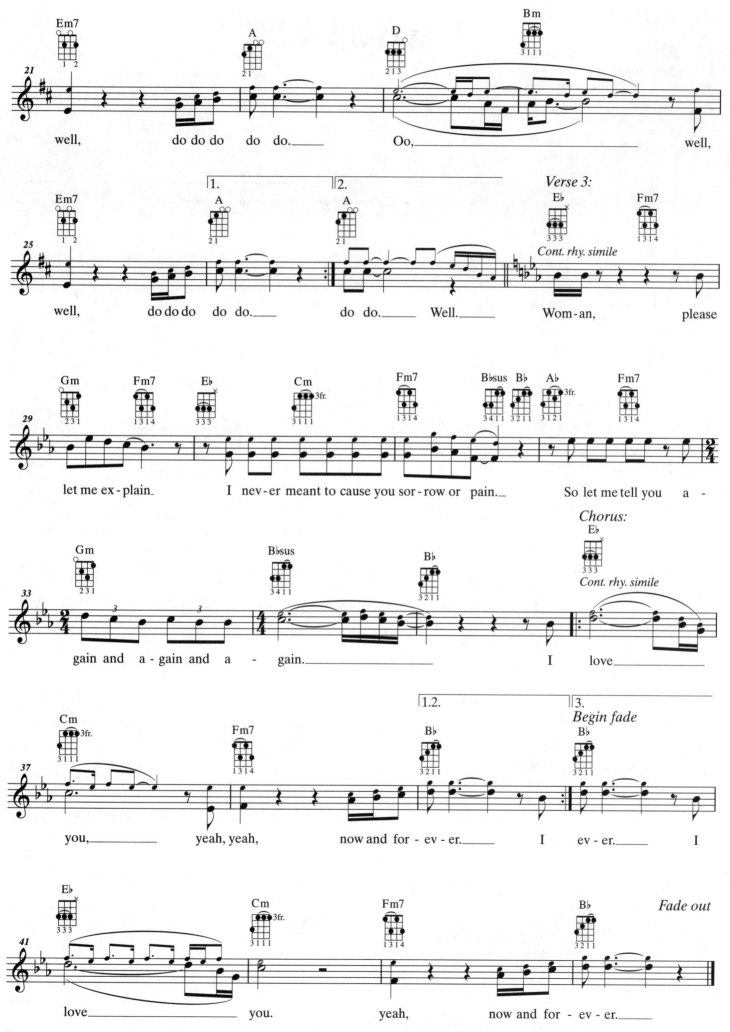

TABLATURE EXPLANATION

TAB illustrates the four strings of the ukulele.
Notes and chords are indicated by the placement of fret numbers on each string.

Standard ukulele tuning for soprano, concert, and tenor models is G–C–E–A with the fourth string tuned a whole step lower than the open 1st string.

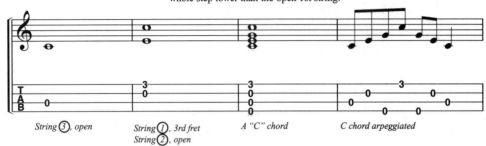

String ③, *open*   *String* ①, *3rd fret*   A "C" chord   C chord arpeggiated
                      String ②, *open*

Alternate Tuning:
Some players (including Israel "Iz" Kamakawiwoʻole) tune their fourth string down one octave from standard ukulele (similar to the first four strings of a guitar with a capo on the 5th fret).

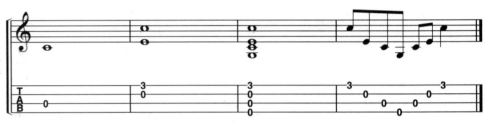

ARTICULATIONS

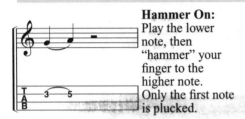

Hammer On:
Play the lower note, then "hammer" your finger to the higher note. Only the first note is plucked.

Pull Off:
Play the higher note with your first finger already in position on the lower note. Pull your finger off the first note with a strong downward motion that plucks the string—sounding the lower note.

Legato Slide:
Play the first note and, keeping pressure applied on the string, slide up to the second note. The diagonal line shows that it is a slide and not a hammer-on or a pull-off.

P.M. - - - - - -

Palm Mute:
The notes are muted (muffled) by placing the palm of the pick hand lightly on the strings, just in front of the bridge.

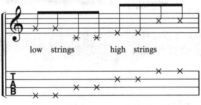

low strings   high strings

Muted Strings:
A percussive sound is produced by striking the strings while laying the fret hand across them.

HARMONICS

harm.   harm.

Natural Harmonic:
A finger of the fret hand lightly touches the string at the note indicated in the TAB and is plucked by the pick producing a bell-like sound called a harmonic.

RHYTHM SLASHES

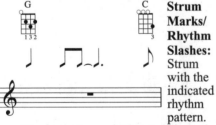

Strum Marks/ Rhythm Slashes:
Strum with the indicated rhythm pattern. Strum marks can be located above the staff or within the staff.

Single Notes with Rhythm Slashes:
Sometimes single notes are incorporated into a strum pattern. The circled number below is the string and the fret number is above.

PICK DIRECTION

Downstrokes and Upstrokes:
The downstroke is indicated with this symbol ⊓ and the upstroke is indicated with this ∨.

BENDING NOTES

Slight Bend/ Quarter-Tone Bend:
Play the note and bend string sharp.

Half Step:
Play the note and bend string one half step (one fret).